Enlightening Object
Lessons for Children

Robert S. Coombs

BAKER BOOK HOUSE
Grand Rapids, Michigan 49516

ISBN: 0-8010-2567-2

Fourth printing, August 1995

Unless otherwise indicated, Scripture references in this volume are from the Revised Standard Version of the Bible, © Copyright 1946, 1952, 1971, 1973 by Thomas Nelson, Inc., New York. Used by permission.

"Safe and Secure" (chapter 39) by Becky Ragsdale is used by permission.

"Someone to Listen" (chapter 40) by Kristen Franks is used by permission.

"A Handful of Pennies" (chapter 41) by Celeste White is used by permission.

"Making a Joyful Noise" (chapter 42) by Stacy McCoy is used by permission.

"Special Needs" (chapter 43) by Jennie Bunch and Stacy McCoy is used by permission.

Printed in the United States of America

To
Kristen Franks and **Celeste White**
two children
who grew to understand the meaning
of unconditional love

Contents

Introduction   9

Introduction

Including a children's sermon as part of the worship service will add an extremely worthwhile and meaningful dimension to worship. Not only will the children feel that they have an important and vital place in the service, but the adults will also gain new insights to simple and yet profound truths.

As stated in my two other books of children's sermons, *Of Such is the Kingdom: Object Sermons for Children* and *Concise Object Sermons for Children*, a few guidelines are noteworthy regarding the development and delivery of a good children's sermon. Please consider the following suggestions:

1. If possible, have a designated area where you may sit and allow the children to gather around you. This provides the opportunity for closeness, eye-to-eye contact, and comfortable dialogue.
2. Begin each children's sermon in the same manner. This will allow each child to know what to expect and thus should prove relaxing. For

example, I begin with a cheerful "Good Morning." The children have become accustomed to this and respond with a hearty "Good Morning" of their own.

3. A good children's sermon, like all good sermons, has one point and one point only. Many children's sermons suffer greatly because the minister seeks to make more than one point.

4. The children are the intended audience of the sermon. Therefore keep your one point simple and easy to understand for the group you are addressing. (The adults will still benefit greatly from the simple truth expressed!)

5. Make your point in two to three minutes. Since a child's attention span is relatively short, even the very best sermon can be ruined by the failure to keep it brief.

6. Encourage interaction. The richest joy of this special time of worship will be the response of the children in your group. The opportunity to participate speaks directly to a child's worth. The feelings of self-worth and importance given to a child in this setting may well carry into adulthood.

7. Enjoy yourself. Preparation and delivery of good children's sermons will bring such a worthwhile variety of results, they could well become a book in their own right.

These lessons have been designed primarily for children ages four to eight.

Train up a child in the way he should go,
and
when he is old he will not depart from it.
Proverbs 22:6

1

What a Match!

Text: "If I speak in the tongues of men and of angels, but have not love, I am a noisy gong or a clanging cymbal" (1 Cor. 13:1).

Object: Mismatched socks

Theme: What we say and what we do should always match.

The strangest thing is happening to me today. Everybody keeps looking at me and, believe it or not, some people have even been giggling behind my back. Can any of you tell me why? [*A quick response should be forthcoming.*] Oh, my goodness, I can't believe it. You are right. My socks don't match! One is [*Point to the sock.*] white and the other is [*Point to the other sock.*] gray. No wonder everybody has been giggling behind my back. I do look ridiculous.

Come to think of it, there is another way we all can look ridiculous. We all look ridiculous when what we say does not match what we do. For example, when I say something like "I love you" and then refuse to help you when you need my help, my actions and my words do not match. That's sad because pretty soon everybody knows how ridiculous I am being and some may even giggle behind my back.

Having socks that match sure is important. But, boys and girls, matching what we say and what we do is even more important.

Dear God, help us to match what we say and what we do. Amen.

2

On Call

Text: "In everything by prayer and supplication with thanksgiving let your requests be made known to God" (Phil. 4:6b).

Object: Beeper

Theme: God is always there, ready to listen to us whenever we need to talk.

This morning I have a rather strange-looking object with me. Perhaps some of you will recognize it, especially if your mom or dad has one. Can anyone tell me what this is? [*Allow the children to respond. If no one guesses correctly, provide the answer.*] Right. This is a beeper. What is a beeper? [*Allow the children to share their answers.*] This is such a smart group. You are exactly right. A beeper beeps whenever someone is trying to call you on a telephone.

Suppose you would like to call a friend. No matter where your friend may be you can always reach him if he has a beeper. All you have to do is dial the number on the telephone and the beeper will beep like this [*Push the beeper button to demonstrate.*] and then your friend will know you are trying to call. Whenever your friend hears this sound, he can go to the nearest phone and give you a call.

Did you know, boys and girls, there is someone who is always there, ready to listen to you? You don't even have to have a beeper to reach him. Can anyone tell me whom I am talking about? [*Allow the children to respond.*] Right. God is always there, ready to listen to us whenever we need to talk. No matter where we are, no matter what we are doing, we can talk to God, and he will be ready and willing to listen.

I am happy we have beepers so we can talk to our friends whenever we need to. But I am even happier we have God to talk to whenever we need to. Let's talk to God right now.

Dear God, thank you for always being there, ready to listen to us whenever we need to talk. Amen.

Money in the Bank

Text: "Yet thou hast made him little less than God, and dost crown him with glory and honor" (Ps. 8:5).

Object: Piggy bank

Theme: Each child is more important than all of the money in the world.

As you can see, I have a rather large piggy bank with me. How many of you have a piggy bank or some other kind of bank at home? [*Allow the children to respond.*] Why do you put money in your piggy bank? [*Allow the children to respond.*] Right. Piggy banks keep all of your money in one place. Then when you need some money you know exactly where to find it. But why do we need money? [*Allow the children to give some examples of how money can be used.*]

Money is valuable because it can buy so many different things, especially when you have lots of money like the amount in this big piggy bank. Did you know that even though money is valuable it is not nearly as valuable as you? Even if we had enough money to fill up this room from the top to the bottom, all of that money would not be nearly as valuable as one of you. In fact each of you is more valuable than all of the money in the world.

Let's thank God for making us so valuable.

Dear God, thank you for making us so valuable. Amen.

On Track

Text: "Teach me thy way, O LORD;" (Ps. 27:11a).

Object: Model train

Theme: Staying on track for God.

Without a doubt, my favorite toy when I was your age was my train. I could spend hours and hours and hours playing with my train set. Do any of you have a train? [*Allow the children to respond.*] Several of you do. Do you enjoy playing with your train? [*Allow the children to share.*] It's great to know so many of you love playing with trains.

As you can see, I have a rather nice engine, coal car, and caboose with me. In fact, these are the same cars and engine I played with as a child. When we look underneath these cars, what do we see? [*Allow the children to answer.*] Exactly. Wheels—many, many wheels. Some of you who are experienced train engineers (that's what we call the person who drives the train) know how important it is for these wheels to stay on the track. What happens if the train wheels come off the track? [*Allow the children to respond.*] Right. The train stops or it might even crash. But if the train wheels stay on the track, the train can go

18

and go and go. So it is very important for a train to stay on the track.

Did you know that it is even more important for you and I to be on track? Of course, we do not run on a track like a train, but we can be on track for God. If we do what God wants us to do, like being loving, kind, and thoughtful, we can stay on track for God and then run and run and run for him. If we do not do what God wants us to do, like saying unkind words, being mean, or doing ugly things, then it is like being off track. Then we cannot go anywhere for God.

Let's ask God to help us stay on track.

Dear God, help us stay on track so we can run and run and run for you. Amen.

5

Needed Rest

Text: "'Come to me, all who labor and are heavy laden, and I will give you rest'" (Matt. 11:28).

Object: Pillow

Theme: Jesus will give us the rest we need.

I was a little concerned that I might get tired during church today so I brought my pillow with me just in case I need to lie down. Do you think that is a good idea? [*Allow the children to respond.*] You are right. Church is not the place to try to sleep. Where would be a good place to sleep? [*Allow the children to respond.*] Of course, the best place to sleep is at home in your bed.

Have you ever been so tired because you ran and played all day that you could hardly wait to get into bed and lay your head down on your fluffy, soft pillow? [*Children should readily agree that they occasionally get this tired.*] When you are that tired and need your rest, there is nothing quite like your own pillow. It makes you feel good all over because you know your pillow will help give you the rest you need.

Sometimes we get tired, not because we have run and played too much, but because we have too many problems. Jesus once told us that if we should ever get tired because we were having too many problems, we should come to him and he will give us rest. When we go to Jesus because of our problems, he makes us feel better, and then we know we can get the rest we need.

Dear God, thank you for Jesus who gives us the rest we need when we are having too many problems. Amen.

Someone's at the Door

Text: "Behold, I stand at the door and knock; if any one hears my voice and opens the door, I will come in to him and eat with him, and he with me" (Rev. 3:20).

Object: Door knocker

Theme: Jesus wants to come into our hearts so we can share our lives with him.

The other day I went to a friend's house, and guess what? I could not get in. First I checked the front door. It was locked. Then I checked the back door and *it* was locked. Both doors to his house were locked. Then I started thinking, *maybe I am doing this all wrong. Maybe I should go to the front door and use this.* Can anyone tell me what this is? [*Allow the children to respond.*] Right. This is a door knocker. And what is a door knocker attached to? [*Allow the children to respond.*] Of course, a door knocker is attached to a door. Why is a door knocker attached to a door? [*Allow the children to explain.*] This is such a smart group, I should have had you with me. When you knock on the door with the door knocker like this [*Use the door knocker.*] someone inside the house will hear the knocking sound and then come to answer the door. That is exactly what I did, and guess what:

in a few moments my friend came to the door and let me come inside, and then we were able to have a wonderful time together.

Jesus once said that he stands at the door to our hearts and knocks because he wants to come inside. Of course our hearts do not have a door like a house. What Jesus meant was that like a friend lets another friend into his or her house so they can be together, Jesus wants to come into our hearts so we can share our lives with him. Allowing Jesus to share our lives means that we will be able to have wonderful times together.

Dear God, help us to open the door to our heart so we can share wonderful times together with Jesus. Amen.

7

More Precious than Diamonds

Text: "Come to him, to that living stone, rejected by men but in God's sight chosen and precious" (1 Peter 2:4).

Object: Diamond ring

Theme: Jesus is more precious than all the diamonds in the world.

I have a ring on my finger that I usually do not wear. Can anyone guess which ring that might be? [*Allow the children to respond.*] Right. The reason I do not wear this ring is because it belongs to my wife, Janet. I gave it to her eleven years ago—that's before most of you were born! I wonder if anyone might be able to guess why I gave this ring to Janet. [*Allow the children to guess.*] This is a smart group. I gave this ring to Janet on the day I asked her to marry me. That was a very special day for me, and I wanted to give her something very nice to show her how much I loved her. The nicest thing I could think of was a diamond ring. Why do you suppose diamonds are so special? [*The children should give several ideas.*]

Diamonds are special because they are very rare or hard to find. That's why we never find diamonds just lying in the backyard alongside of other stones. Since there are not many diamonds in the world, the diamonds we have are very, very precious. In fact, they are the most precious stones in the whole world.

Let me share with you something that is even more precious than this diamond. Jesus is more precious than this diamond or, in fact, all the diamonds in the whole wide world put together. Jesus is precious because there never has been or never will be another person like him. He is God's precious Son who came to tell us about God in a way no other person has ever been able to do. Let's thank God for sending us Jesus who is more precious than all the diamonds in the world.

Dear God, thank you for Jesus who is more precious than all the diamonds in the world. Amen.

The Right Light

> **Text:** "Arise, shine; for your light has come, and the glory of the Lord has risen upon you" (Isa. 60:1).
>
> **Object:** Children with their eyes closed tightly
>
> **Theme:** God's light will show us the right way to go.

I would like all of you to close your eyes as tightly as you can. Please keep your eyes closed until I say it is okay to open them. Tell me, what can you see? [*Allow the children to respond.*] Nothing? Nothing at all? Right. If your eyes are closed very tightly, everything is dark. What if I were to ask you to run and play or to find your mother or father with your eyes closed? Would that be a good idea? [*A quick response should be in order.*] Right. Running and playing or trying to find someone in the dark is not a good idea. When it is so dark you cannot see anything, it is pretty scary to move.

Now open your eyes. Because the light is coming into your eyes you can see everything. If I were to ask you to run and play or try to find your mom or dad, none of you would have a problem doing that.

With light we easily find the way so we really do not need to worry about getting hurt.

Sometimes we think of God as light because living without God is like living in the darkness. Without God, finding our way through life is like walking around with our eyes tightly closed. That can be pretty scary. But with God's light there is really no reason to be scared because we can be sure that he will show us the right way to go.

Dear God, thank you for being our light and for showing us the right way to go. Amen.

A Winning Team

> **Text:** "Teacher, I will follow you wherever you go" (Matt. 8:19b).
> **Object:** Tickets
> **Theme:** Through Jesus, we join God's team.

Hidden away in my coat pocket I have something that is very valuable. [*Bring the object into view.*] You may be wondering what is so valuable about two little pieces of colorful paper with words written all over them. Can anyone tell me what I have in my hand? [*Allow the children to respond. Most likely, several of the children will be aware of what you hold.*] Right. These are tickets. But, they are not just any old tickets. They are tickets to a Big Orange [or other area game of importance] football game. Because our team has been winning so much this year, these tickets are very valuable. It seems that everyone loves being a part of a winning team.

In the Bible Jesus invites all of us to be part of God's winning team. Our ticket to God's winning team comes when we accept Jesus into our hearts. Through Jesus, we join God's team and we can be sure that as members of God's team we can learn to do winning things like telling the truth, treating others with kindness, and lending a helping hand.

Let's thank God for allowing us to join his winning team through Jesus.

Dear God, thank you for allowing us to join your winning team through Jesus. Amen.

10

Over the Hill

> **Text:** "'He who conquers shall have this heritage, and I will be his God and he shall be my son'" (Rev. 21:7).
>
> **Object:** Bicycle
>
> **Theme:** Our lives can be a lot like riding a bicycle up and down hills.

Of all the wonderful things to do in this world, riding a bicycle has to be one of the best. How many of you enjoy riding a bicycle? [*Allow the children to respond.*] What do you think is the hardest thing about riding a bicycle? [*Allow the children to share some ideas. When someone mentions peddling uphill, continue with the message.*] I agree with (Name). Peddling uphill is always a lot of hard work. Especially if the hill is very, very long. Sometimes it seems to take forever to reach the top. What do you think is the easiest thing about riding a bicycle? [*After discussing the difficulty of peddling uphill, several of the children should mention that riding downhill is easy.*] Riding downhill is the easiest, and if the hill is steep enough you don't even have to peddle. You can just coast all the way down the hill and enjoy the breeze blowing in your face.

As much as I like going downhill, I understand the importance of going uphill. Even though going uphill is harder, without the climb to the top of the hill, there is no way to enjoy going down the other side. Sometimes when I am having an especially hard time going uphill, I start thinking about going down the other side and that gives me the energy I need to make it to the top.

Our lives can be a lot like riding a bicycle up and down hills. When we are having problems in school, at home, or with a friend, it is like peddling uphill. Sometimes it feels like our problems will never end. The thing to do when we are feeling as though our problems will never end is to remember that sooner or later they will. Like riding a bike to the top of the hill, if we remember that problems do end we will have enough energy to reach the top and then can enjoy coasting down the other side.

Dear God, help us to remember that our problems will end. Amen.

11

The Domino Effect

Text: "Love one another with brotherly affection; outdo one another in showing honor" (Rom. 12:10).

Object: Dominoes

Theme: Everything we do or say has a way of touching someone else.

How many of you have ever played the game of dominoes? [*Begin setting up the dominoes and continue with the message.*] I love to play the game of dominoes, but I enjoy setting them up on their ends and making interesting patterns even more. Can you tell what pattern I am making today? [*Allow the children to respond.*] Right. This pattern is in the shape of an *S.* Do you think if I knock over this domino, [*Point to the domino at the beginning of the pattern.*] this domino [*Point to the last domino.*] will fall over? [*Answers to this question may vary depending on whether or not the children have ever seen the domino effect.*] Why? [*Allow the children to explain.*] You are exactly right. The first domino in line will knock over the second domino in line which will knock over the third domino which will knock over the fourth domino until finally each domino in line is knocked over so that the last one in line falls. Would you like to see if this really works? [*An enthusiastic "yes" should be forthcoming!*] Let's watch. [*Knock over the first domino and watch the domino effect with the children.*]

Watching the dominoes fall is a lot of fun but it also teaches us a special lesson. Did you know that everything we say or do really touches someone else? Just as the first domino touched the second domino which touched the third domino and then the fourth and fifth and so on, whatever we say or do has a way of touching someone else and then someone else is touched, then someone else, and so on. Let's try something that will show you what I mean. I am going to hold (Name's) hand. Now (Name), you hold someone else's hand. (Name), since (Name) took your hand, you take someone else's hand. [*Continue to have the children join hands until the entire group is holding hands.*] Tell me, how does it make you feel to be holding hands? [*The children will respond with some form of positive response. Use that response and continue.*] From the first person to the last person, joining hands has been a way of touching each other with our love just as the dominoes touched each other.

Remember, everything we do or say has a way of touching someone else. Let's ask God's help to touch others with our love.

Dear God, help us to touch others with our love. Amen.

12

Soaking Up God's Love

Text: "The heavens are telling the glory of God; and the firmament proclaims his handiwork" (Ps. 19:1).

Object: Sponge

Theme: Like sponges, we can soak up God's love.

How many of you have ever helped your mom or dad wash the family car? [*Allow the children to share some of their experiences of helping to wash the family car.*] Part of the fun of washing the car is getting to use one of these. What is this called? [*Allow the children to respond.*] Of course, this is a sponge. How does a sponge work? [*Allow the children to explain.*] This is such a smart group. The sponge does help move the water from the bucket to the car. Just as you said, it does that by soaking up water from the bucket.

Sometimes when I am washing my car (with my children's help, of course), I think of how wonderful it would be to be like this sponge—but not to soak up water. Instead, I would like to do as good a job soaking up God's love as this sponge does soaking up water. Soaking up God's love should be as easy for me as it is for this sponge to soak up water. That's because everywhere I look I can see and feel God's love. The warm sunshine, a gentle breeze, the touch of your hand, and a kind word from a friend are all part of God's love. Let's try to be like a sponge and every day do our very best to soak up God's love.

Dear God, help us to do our best to soak up your love every day. Amen.

13

Hooray for M & M's

Text: "And God saw everything that he had made, and behold, it was very good" (Gen. 1:31a).

Object: M & M's

Theme: Part of what makes each of us interesting is that we have different colors of hair, of eyes, and of skin.

I am glad to see all of you here today, and when you see what I have, you will be especially glad you are here! Can you see what is inside my bowl? [*A quick response should be in order.*] Of course, M & M's. Do any of you like to eat M & M's? [*Another enthusiastic response should be forthcoming.*] Well, to tell you the truth I don't like M & M's. I LOVE M & M's. In fact, it just about takes all the willpower I have to sit here and not gobble up all of these M & M's. I love the green ones [*Eat it.*] and the red ones [*Eat it.*] and the yellow ones [*Eat it.*] and the brown ones [*Eat it.*]. To tell you the truth I have never tasted any color of M & M's that I did not love. I believe that having so many different colors makes eating M & M's just that much more fun. Just think of how boring it would be if all M & M's came in the same color. Eating just green M & M's could not possibly be as much fun as eating all of these wonderful colors.

Of course, M & M's are not the only things in this world that are better because they come in different colors. I think people are more exciting because we come in different colors. Can you imagine how boring it would be if everyone had the same color hair, eyes, and skin? Part of what makes each of us interesting is that we have different colors of hair, eyes, and skin.

I am going to give each of you a package of M & M's to eat after church. As you are eating your different color M & M's, remember that as much fun as that makes for enjoying M & M's, it makes for even more fun when enjoying people.

Dear God, thank you for making each of us different. Amen.

14

Hooray for M & M's Again

Text: "There is neither Jew nor Greek, there is
neither slave nor free, there is neither male
nor female; for you are all one in Christ
Jesus" (Gal. 3:28).

Object: M & M's

Theme: No matter what color we are on the
outside, we are all the same on the inside.

Note: This lesson should be used as a sequel
to lesson 13.

[*Bring the bowl of M & M's into view.*] I can see that
many of you simply cannot believe your eyes. We
had a bowlful of M & M's last Sunday and we have
another bowlful of M & M's this Sunday. Isn't that
wonderful? All of you seem as eager to dig into the
M & M's as you were last week.

Last Sunday we talked about M & M's being especially exciting because they come in so many different _____. [*Allow the children to fill in the blank
with their response.*] Right. Colors. And, then, remember I said that part of what makes people so exciting
is that we come in so many different colors.

Can you tell me what is inside this green M & M?
[*The children should quickly point out that chocolate is
inside.*] How about this red M & M? [*Allow the chil-*

dren to respond.] How about this brown M & M? [*Allow the children to respond.*] How about this yellow M & M? [*Allow the children to respond.*] You mean, chocolate is inside every M & M? [*Allow the children to respond.*] That means that every M & M is exactly the same on the inside. No matter what color they may be on the outside, they are all the same on the inside.

That's true, not just with M & M's, but with people also. We may have different colors of skin or eyes or hair, but on the inside we are all the same. What I mean is that we all have the same needs—the need to be loved; the need to be treated with kindness; the need to be accepted; and especially the need to have Jesus in our hearts.

I am thankful for M & M's. They have taught us two important lessons. Enjoy your M & M's and remember the lessons you have learned from them.

Dear God, help us to remember that no matter what color we are on the outside, we are all the same on the inside. Amen.

15

What Talent!

Text: "'Master, you delivered to me five talents; here I have made five talents more.' His master said to him, 'Well done, good and faithful servant; you have been faithful over a little, I will set you over much; enter into the joy of your master'" (Matt. 25:20b–21).

Object: Coupon

Theme: We should use our talents.

Now that it is spring and every day seems to be getting warmer and warmer, I find myself thinking a lot about ice cream. Do you all like ice cream? [*An enthusiastic response should be forthcoming!*] I like ice cream too—especially chocolate ice cream. I guess that's my favorite, although I love just about every kind of ice cream made. What is your favorite flavor? [*Allow the children to share their favorites.*] Just hearing all of you talk about those wonderful flavors is making me anxious to go out and get a chocolate ice cream cone. Wouldn't that be great? Of course, we can't do that right now, but I believe I have the next best thing to an ice cream cone. Can anyone tell me what this is? [*Allow the children to respond.*] Right. This is a coupon. What is a coupon? [*Allow the chil-*

dren to tell you what it is.] You all are so smart. You not only know a lot about ice cream but also about how coupons work. Just as you said, all I have to do is take this coupon to [*Name of store.*] and they will give me a free ice cream cone of whatever flavor I choose.

If I put this coupon in my pocket, and never take it to [*Name of store.*], do you think my coupon will be very useful? [*Allow the children to respond.*] Right, as nice as this coupon is, it really is not any good at all unless I use it.

The same is true about our talents. Our talents are the special gifts that God gives us to use in our lives. Some of you have musical talent, some of you can run especially fast, some of you are very smart. Whatever talent God has given you, it is important to use it. If we don't use our talents, then it is like not using a valuable coupon. That would be pretty foolish.

I have a [*Name of ice cream parlor.*] coupon for each of you. Make sure you put your coupon to good use and get a great ice cream cone. When you are eating your ice cream, remember the gifts God has given to you, your special talents, and remember to put them to good use.

Dear God, thank you for the gift of our talents. Help us to use them. Amen.

16

A Better Eye Test

Text: "'Blessed are your eyes, for they see'" (Matt. 13:16a).

Object: Eyeglasses

Theme: Just as glasses help us see better with our eyes, Jesus can help us see better with our hearts.

The object I have with me today is very important for many people. Can you tell me what these are? [*Allow the children to respond.*] Right. These are eyeglasses. Why are glasses important? [*Allow the children to explain the importance of glasses.*] Glasses are important because they can help us to see better. Why is it important to see well? [*Allow the children to provide some reasons.*] Of course seeing well is important for just about everything we do—like reading a book, playing a game, drawing a picture, or watching a pretty sunset.

Seeing well is not just important with our eyes, it is also important with our hearts. Did you know that our hearts can see? What I mean by seeing with our hearts is seeing special times when we can help other people. Jesus can help us see better with our hearts in much the same way that glasses help us see better with our eyes. When we visit a grandmother who is lonely, care for a friend who is sick, listen to a mom who is sad, or help Dad get a special job done, we are seeing with our hearts.

It's wonderful to have glasses that help us to see better with our eyes. But it is even more wonderful to have Jesus who helps us see better with our hearts.

Dear God, thank you for Jesus who helps us see better with our hearts. Amen.

17

Sharing the Light

Text: "For so the Lord had commanded us, saying, 'I have set you to be a light for the Gentiles, that you may bring salvation to the uttermost parts of the earth'" (Acts 13:47).

Object: Candle

Theme: No matter how much goodness you give away, you still have just as much goodness inside.

I have a candle for each of you. [*Hand out a candle to each child. (Birthday size would be appropriate.) You and one other adult should have a large candle mounted on a base to protect from potential wax drips.*] I am going to light my candle so we can talk about its light. When you get home, you may light your candle with your mom or dad and tell them what you have learned today.

[*Lighting your candle, ask the following question.*] Tell me, what do you like about candles? [*Children should be quick to provide a variety of answers such as: candles make me think of birthdays; candles smell good; candles are pretty; candles glow in the dark, and so forth.*] I like all the things you said about candles. There is something else that I think is very special about candles.

44

What would happen if I used the light on my candle to light my friend's candle? [*Allow the children to respond.*] Some of you do not seem quite sure what would happen. Let's try it and see. [*Using your candle, light the candle held by the other adult.*] What happened to my light? [*Allow the children to respond.*] Right. I still have the light on my candle. It is still shining brightly. What happened to my friend's candle? [*Allow the children to respond.*] Right. Now it is burning brightly. Isn't that amazing? I was able to share my light with another candle and I still have just as much light as before.

Let me share something with you that is even more amazing. Did you know that you can share your goodness with others and still have just as much goodness inside? No matter how much goodness you give away by doing kind deeds like being nice to your sister or brother, cleaning your room, helping fix supper, or cheering up a sad friend, you still have just as much goodness inside.

This week, try giving away some of your goodness. You will find that by next week you will still have just as much goodness inside.

Dear God, help us to give our goodness to others. Amen.

18

Huh???

Text: "And he said, 'He who has ears to hear, let him hear'" (Mark 4:9).

Object: Hearing aid

Theme: Jesus helps us listen with our hearts.

Good morning. [*Allow the children to respond.*] I'm sorry. What did you say? [*Bending your ear forward, as if you did not hear them, listen for another response.* The children should produce a somewhat louder "Good Morning."] Really, I was just kidding. I can hear you all loud and clear. But did you know there are some people who really do have a hard time hearing? For people who cannot hear well, this can be very helpful. Can anyone tell me what this is? [*Produce the hearing aid for the children to see. Most likely, one of the children will know this object. If not, supply the answer after a few moments.*] You are such a smart group. You are right. This is a hearing aid. What does a hearing aid do? [*Allow the children to respond.*] Exactly. A hearing aid takes sound and makes it louder. With the louder sound coming into the person's ear, the person can hear better.

Some people may need to hear better with their ears, but many people need to hear better with their hearts. What I mean by hearing with our hearts is listening for chances to love one another. Who is our best teacher for loving one another? [*Allow the children to respond.*] Yes. Jesus is our best teacher. He is sort of like a hearing aid that helps us listen better with our hearts. Jesus helps us listen for chances to love one another. Can you think of some of the ways Jesus helps us listen for chances to love one another? [*Allow the children to share a few ideas.*]

Let's thank God for giving us Jesus who helps us listen with our hearts.

Dear God, thank you for Jesus who helps us to listen with our hearts. Amen.

19

Needed Protection

Text: "Put on the whole armor of God, that you may be able to stand against the wiles of the devil" (Eph. 6:11).

Object: Football shoulder pads

Theme: Jesus gives us the protection we need to face our hurts.

Imagine how much fun it would be to be a great football player. Wouldn't it be fun to be able to run fast as lightning down the field and catch a football and then run for a touchdown? Then, of course, you would get to hear the crowd cheer. Wouldn't that be great? [*Allow the children to respond. A few may have a story about themselves or their dads playing football.*]

Of course, there is something about football that doesn't seem like much fun at all—getting hit. I don't think I would like that part of football because I do not care for being hurt and I am sure that every time you get hit, it hurts. Do you like to be hurt? [*A quick response should be in order.*]

In case you ever do play football, it is important to wear these. Can anyone tell me what I have? [*Allow the children to respond.*] Right; these are shoulder pads. They fit on your shoulders like this. [*Demonstrate.*] Why do you suppose football players wear shoulder pads? [*Allow the children to respond.*] Right; the pads give the player added protection. No matter how big or strong a football player may be, he still needs the protection that shoulder pads give.

Of course, football is not the only place we can get hurt. I think that the hurts we feel when we have a fight with a friend, when a special pet dies, or when we do something we know we shouldn't, can hurt even more than being hit by a football player. Of course football pads would not help for these kind of hurts but Jesus can. Like football pads, Jesus can help protect us when we are hit with hurts like a fight with a friend, the sadness of losing a pet, or suffering the outcome of a bad decision or choice.

Let's thank God for Jesus who gives us the protection we need to face our hurts.

Dear God, thank you for Jesus who gives us the protection we need to face our hurts. Amen.

20

Working Together

> **Text:** "For we are God's fellow workers; you are God's field, God's building" (1 Cor. 3:9 NIV).
>
> **Object:** Ant farm
>
> **Theme:** It is important for us to work together.

On a hot summer day, have you ever sat on your driveway or on the sidewalk and watched ants? [*Allow the children to respond.*] I have and I think it is pretty fascinating—especially if you are sitting near an anthill and watching a whole bunch of ants working together. In fact, I like watching ants so much that I have an ant farm. Looking through this glass you can see hundreds of ants busily working together making tunnels through the dirt, carrying food from one place to another, and cleaning the space where they sleep.

Can you imagine what it would be like if one ant had to do all this work? Do you think that one ant could make all the tunnels, carry all the food, and do all the cleaning? [*Allow the children to respond.*] No? Why not? [*The children will point out that this is too much work for one ant.*] You are right. Making all these tunnels, carrying all the food, and doing all the cleaning is too much work for one ant. Do you think it is too much work for one hundred ants? [*The children will point out that one hundred ants can handle this much work.*] Sure. If one hundred ants work together, they can handle all the work.

The same is true, not just for ants, but for all of us. Do you think one person could do all the work in our church? Could one person do all the teaching, all the music, all the cleaning of our building? [*The children should be shaking their heads no by this point.*] Of course not. Do you think it is too much work if everybody in our church works together? [*The children will point out that if everybody works together, we can do the work.*] Sure. If all of us work together, we can handle all the work.

Next time you see ants crawling along the sidewalk, think about how they all work together. And then remember how important it is for us to work together.

Dear God, thank you for ants that teach us the importance of working together. Amen.

21

A Vital Supply

Text: "The LORD will keep
your going out and your coming in
from this time forth and for evermore"
(Ps. 121:8).

Object: Skin-diving tank

Theme: We need God as much as the air we
breathe.

How many of you enjoy swimming? [*An enthusiastic response should be forthcoming.*] Have you ever imagined what it would be like to stay underwater for a long time and swim anywhere you would like? [*Allow the children to respond.*] If you had the object I have with me this morning and knew how to use it, you would be able to swim underwater for more than an hour without coming to the surface to take a breath. Can anyone tell me what this object is? [*Most likely, at least one child will recognize this object. If not, supply the answer.*] Yes. This is called an air tank. You wear it on your back, like this. [*Demonstrate.*] What do you suppose is inside this tank? [*Allow the children to respond.*] Right. Air is in the tank and air, of course, is what we need to breathe. So if you put this hose up to your mouth while you are underwater, you can breathe the air from the tank.

What do you suppose would happen if you were deep under the water and all the air ran out of this tank? [*Allow the children to respond.*] You are right. You would be in big trouble because you would no longer be able to breathe. As long as you are under the water, your life really depends on your tank giving you the air you need to breathe.

Thinking of how much we need air to breathe reminds me of how much we need God in our lives. Without God our lives are in as much trouble as when we are underwater without any air. We need God as much as we need the air that we breathe. And like the air we breathe, we can be sure that God will always be there for each of us.

Dear God, help us to remember that we need you as much as the air we breathe. Amen.

22

Let's Talk

Text: "Pray constantly" (1 Thess. 5:17).
Object: Sign language
Theme: Prayer is our special way of talking with God.

I have a friend with me who can talk with her hands. [*If you do not have someone in your church who knows sign language, you may want to learn a simple phrase, such as, "I love you," or use a sign-language chart as your object.*] My friend would like to share something with you in sign language. [*Have the person communicate a few simple thoughts.*] Kristen is saying that she is very glad to be with us today. She also says you are a group of beautiful children. We are glad to have you with us also, Kristen.

Why do you suppose Kristen uses sign language? [*Allow the children to explain.*] Right. She uses sign language to talk with persons who cannot hear. However, they can watch her hands and see the words that she is saying.

Sign language is our special way of talking with people who cannot hear. What is our special way of talking with God whom we cannot see? [*At least one child should be able to provide the correct answer.*] Of course, prayer is our special way of talking with God. When we talk with God through prayer, even though we cannot see him, we can be sure that God listens carefully to every word we say.

Let's talk to God right now and thank him for giving us a special way to talk to him.

Dear God, thank you for giving us a special way to talk to you. Amen.

23

Together We Build

> **Text:** "For we are his workmanship, created in Christ Jesus for good works, which God prepared beforehand, that we should walk in them" (Eph. 2:10).
>
> **Object:** Toolbox
>
> **Theme:** God needs all of us to get his work done.

How many of you have ever helped build something? [*Children should eagerly tell the things they have helped to build.*] Whenever you are building something like a toy box, a dollhouse, shelves for your books, or whatever, having a box filled with tools is very important. Let's take a look inside my toolbox to see what we have. Maybe you can even name some of the tools. What is this? [*Show the children a hammer.*] Of course, this is a hammer. What is a hammer used for? [*Allow the children to explain.*] What is this? [*Show the children a drill.*] Right. This is a drill. What is a drill used for? [*Allow the children to explain.*] What is this? [*Show the children a screwdriver.*] Yes. This is a screwdriver. What is a screwdriver used for? [*Allow the children to explain.*] What is this? [*Show the children a wrench.*] Yes. This is a wrench. What is a wrench used for? [*Allow the children to explain.*]

As you can see, there are many different tools in my toolbox. Each tool does something different, but every tool is important for getting the job done.

In much the same way I need all of my tools to get my work done, God needs all of you to get his work done. Looking at each of you, I can see that each of you is different. Like a hammer, a screwdriver, a wrench, or a drill, every one of you has something special to offer. Some of you are especially good singers, some of you are very friendly, some of you are good listeners. Whatever is special about you is important. When all of you work together, each doing your own special part, God's work gets done.

Dear God, help us each to do our part in getting your work done. Amen.

24

Sweetness

Text: "How sweet are thy words to my taste, sweeter than honey to my mouth!" (Ps. 119:103).

Object: Kool-Aid and sugar

Theme: Adding a little sweetness in all that we do makes our lives so much sweeter.

When you come inside on a hot summer day after playing in the sun for hours, how many of you like to drink a big glass of Kool-Aid? [*Allow the children to respond.*] I like Kool-Aid too. Since today is a hot day, I brought some Kool-Aid for us to share this morning. Would you like some? [*Allow the children to respond.*] (Name), please taste a glass of my Kool-Aid and tell me if it is not the best you have ever tasted. [*The Kool-Aid you have prepared should not have sugar added.*] It's not? What's wrong with my Kool-Aid? [*Allow the child to respond. The child should respond that the drink tastes sour or funny.*] It's sour? Let me taste it and see. [*Taste the Kool-Aid.*] You are right. This Kool-Aid is sour. No wonder! I forgot to add the sugar.

Luckily I happen to have some sugar with me. Let's put in a little sugar and see if that makes a difference. [*Add the appropriate amount of sugar to the*

Kool-Aid and stir. Then taste the Kool-Aid.] Goodness, what a wonderful difference a little sugar has made. (Name), now try this Kool-Aid and tell me if it is not the best Kool-Aid you have ever tasted. [*Allow the child to taste the Kool-Aid and respond.*]

Like adding a little sugar to Kool-Aid makes it taste so much sweeter, adding a little sweetness in all that we do makes our lives so much sweeter. We can add sweetness by remembering to say the magic words *please* and *thank you*, by helping a friend with a problem, or by trying our best to get along with our brother or sister. Whatever way you can find to add sweetness in what you do, you will find that your life will be that much sweeter.

After children's church, I have plenty of Kool-Aid for all of you to drink. As you are drinking it, remember the importance of adding sweetness to all that you do.

Dear God, help us to remember the importance of adding sweetness to all that we do. Amen.

25

All Charged Up

> **Text:** "Even a child makes himself known by his acts, whether what he does is pure and right" (Prov. 20:11).
>
> **Object:** Battery
>
> **Theme:** We should put our energy to good use.

With all the different toys that cry and laugh, bark and meow, or go backward and forward, it is very important to have plenty of these around the house. Can you tell me what I am holding? [*Allow the children to respond.*] Of course. This is a battery. Why is a battery important for a toy that moves or makes a noise? [*Allow the children to explain.*] This is a smart group. The battery supplies the energy for the toy to work.

A battery by itself is not much good, is it? A battery only becomes useful when it is put into something. Put the battery into the right toy and in a moment the toy can use the energy from the battery to come to life. It's wonderful to have batteries that we can put to good use.

Looking around this group of boys and girls, I can see that this battery is not the only thing that is full of energy. Each one of you is full of energy. It's wonderful to have a group of children filled with energy. But the truth is that all of your energy is not much good to you unless you put it to good use. What are some of the ways you can put your energy to good use? [*Allow the children to give a few examples.*] (Name) says he can put his energy to good use by cleaning his room. (Name) says she can put her energy to good use by reading her Bible. (Name) says he can put his energy to good use by washing the dishes. (Name) says she can put her energy to good use by coming to church every Sunday.

You have thought of some wonderful ways to put your energy to good use. Every time you use a battery, try to think of another way you can put your energy to good use.

Dear God, help us to put our energy to good use. Amen.

26

Being Noticed

Text: "Let us hold fast the confession of our
hope without wavering, for he who
promised is faithful" (Heb. 10:23).

Object: Chameleon

Theme: Sometimes we need to be noticed.

Some of you seem a little afraid to gather around
for our children's sermon today. Don't worry, my little friend will not hurt you. We will keep him inside
the jar. Can anyone tell me what I have inside this
jar? [*Allow the children to respond.*] Right. This is a
lizard. What sort of lizard do you think he is? [*One of
the children might know. If not, supply the correct
answer.*] This is a chameleon. Can you tell me what is
special about a chameleon? [*Allow the children to
respond. Many of the children should know the answer to
this question.*] You are such a smart group. A
chameleon can change color and blend in with his
background. If we put this chameleon on a green
leaf, he would turn _____. [*Allow the children to
supply the answer.*] If we put this chameleon on
brown bark, the chameleon would turn _____.
[*Allow the children to supply the answer.*] Wherever the

chameleon happens to be, he can change color to blend in with his background.

Blending in so you are not noticed is a good habit for a chameleon, but can be a very bad habit for us. Sometimes we need to be noticed. When everybody is taking drugs, do you think you should take drugs too? [*Allow the children to respond.*] Of course not. We need to be noticed by saying *no*. If everyone is being mean to your teacher, should you be mean too? [*Allow the children to respond.*] Of course not. Again, we need to be noticed by saying *no*. If all of your friends decide to steal something, do you think you should steal something too? [*Allow the children to respond.*] Of course not. Again, we need to be noticed by saying *no*.

Let's ask God to help us to be noticed by saying *no* whenever we are asked to do something wrong.

Dear God, help us to say no *whenever we are asked to do wrong. Amen.*

27

Pizza Time

Text: "O LORD, I love the habitation of thy house, and the place where thy glory dwells" (Ps. 26:8).

Object: Pizza

Theme: Our church has a lot to offer each of us.

What is your favorite meal? [*Although there will be a variety of meals mentioned, pizza should be one of the most popular.*] You are making me hungry. Thank goodness I happen to have one of the meals that seems to be the most popular. Can anyone tell me what is inside this box? [*Use an easily recognizable pizza box from a local restaurant.*] Right. Inside this box I have a wonderful pizza. Let's take a peek. [*Open the box for the children to view. I recommend getting a pizza with toppings most children enjoy.*] Doesn't this pizza look delicious? [*Allow the children to respond.*]

What do you like most about pizza? [*Reinforce each answer the children provide.*] (Name) likes the crust. (Name) likes the pepperoni. (Name) likes the tomato sauce. (Name) likes the cheese. Maybe you like all the different ingredients that come together to make a wonderful taste. [*Close the lid to the pizza box and continue.*]

Can you tell me what you like most about our church? [*Reinforce each answer the children provide.*] (Name) likes his Sunday school class. (Name) likes her choir. (Name) likes children's church. (Name) likes coming to church to learn about Jesus. Maybe what you like most about our church is all the different reasons you have for coming. Like a pizza that has a lot to offer each of you, our church has a lot to offer each of you. I hope you will enjoy our church as much as you enjoy pizza.

Dear God, help us to enjoy our church; it offers us so much. Amen.

28

What Goes Around, Comes Around

> **Text:** "Do not be deceived; God is not mocked, for whatever a man sows, that he will also reap" (Gal. 6:7).
>
> **Object:** Boomerang
>
> **Theme:** Love usually comes back to you when you give it away.

I have an object with me that most of you have probably seen at one time or another, but few of you have ever had the chance to play with. Can anyone tell me what this is? [*Bring the boomerang into view.*] Right. This is a boomerang. What is special about a boomerang? [*Allow the children to respond. If they are unable to answer, provide the answer for them.*] When you throw a boomerang away from you, it usually comes back to you. It sort of makes a big circle in the air. I would love to show you how it works, but inside our sanctuary is not a good place. Boomerangs should only be thrown outside.

Have you ever heard someone say, "If you want to be loved, be lovable?" [*Allow the children to respond.*] What do you suppose that means: "If you want to be loved, be lovable?" [*Most likely one of the children will grasp the truth of this statement. Using his/her words, communicate the following thought.*] I see. It's sort of like saying that if you want someone to love you, you should love them. That's just like a boomerang. You throw it away, and usually it comes back. You give love away, and usually it comes back.

This week try giving away some love, and watch love come back to you.

Dear God, help us to give away our love this week. Amen.

29

Like a Flower

Text: "But grow in the grace and knowledge
of our Lord and Savior Jesus Christ" (2
Peter 3:18a).

Object: Flower

Theme: A church provides the right conditions for us to grow.

[*If you have flowers decorating your sanctuary, begin
this message by removing one flower from the arrange-
ment. If you do not use flowers to decorate your sanctuary, bring a flower.*] What kind of flower am I holding? [*Allow the children to respond. An easily
identifiable flower is best.*] Right. This is a rose—a
beautiful, red rose that smells like perfume. Every
Sunday, we have beautiful flowers decorating our
sanctuary. During the summer months it is not so
difficult to understand how we could have flowers in
our sanctuary because there are flowers growing
everywhere. But this is the middle of winter. When
you go outside, there is not a flower in sight. How
do you suppose we have a beautiful, red rose like this
one in the middle of winter? [*If one of the children
knows the correct answer, continue using his or her explanation. If none of the children know the correct answer,
provide the explanation.*] This rose was grown in a spe-

cial type of house called a greenhouse. Can you tell me what is special about a greenhouse? [*Allow the children to respond.*] Right, (Name). Greenhouses are kept at just the right temperature for flowers to grow. Yes, (Name). Inside a greenhouse you can make sure the flowers receive just the right amount of water. (Name's) right too. Flowers can receive just the right amount of light inside a greenhouse. Greenhouses are wonderful because they provide the best possible conditions for a flower to grow.

Just as a greenhouse provides the right conditions for a flower to grow, a church provides the right conditions for you to grow. In church we receive what we need to grow in God's love, to grow in understanding how to help one another, and to grow in our knowledge of God's Word.

Let's thank God, not only for greenhouses that provide the right conditions for flowers to grow, but also for churches that provide the right conditions for us to grow.

Dear God, thank you for greenhouses that provide the right conditions for flowers to grow and for churches that provide the right conditions for us to grow. Amen.

30

Lightening the Load

Text: "Then he said to his disciples, 'The harvest is plentiful, but the laborers are few; pray therefore the Lord of the harvest to send out laborers into his harvest'" (Matt. 9:37–38).

Object: Box of books

Theme: Each person needs to share in the work of the church.

I have a problem. I have this huge box of books that I need to take to my office, but the box is much too heavy for me to lift. Maybe one of you would like to carry the box to my office for me. [*Allow a few children to try to lift the box.*] Goodness. The box is much too heavy for you, too. This is a problem. What can we do? I *must* get all of these books to my office. [*Allow the children to make suggestions. Someone should suggest each person carrying one or two books.*] What a wonderful idea. If we all work together and each carry two books, we can easily take all the books in this box to my office.

Maybe you can help me with another problem. In our church there are hundreds of jobs that need to be done. In fact there are more jobs than there are books in my box. Because there are so many jobs, it seems impossible for one person to do them all—as impossible as one person lifting this box. What do you suppose is the best solution to this problem? [*Allow the children to propose a solution. Someone should suggest the solution of everyone sharing the jobs.*] That is a wonderful idea. If everyone in our church does his or her share of jobs, we can more easily take care of all that needs to be done.

After our prayer, I would appreciate it if each of you would take two books to my office. As you are carrying them, think of how all of us can do our share of the work in God's church.

Dear God, help us to remember that each of us needs to share in the work of your church. Amen.

31

That Special Glow

Text: "'Then the righteous will shine like the sun in the kingdom of their Father'" (Matt. 13:43a).

Object: Glow-in-the-dark toy

Theme: With Jesus in our hearts we can glow with happiness, love, and kindness.

When I was your age, after I turned out my lights to go to bed at night, I could no longer see all the toys in my room. However today many of the toys continue to glow after all the lights are turned off. If we could make our sanctuary dark, we would see that this toy can glow in the dark. Do any of you have toys that glow in the dark? [*The children will mention a variety of toys.*] Why do you suppose some toys glow in the dark? [*Allow the children to suggest answers.*] Right. The toys that glow in the dark have a special chemical in them. No matter how dark it is, the chemical will make the toy glow.

Sometimes we think of Christians as having a special glow. Of course, we do not glow in the dark like a toy, but we can glow with happiness, love, and kindness. Why do you suppose a Christian can glow? [*Allow the children to provide the answer.*] Right. We can glow as Christians because we have Jesus in our hearts. Jesus can make us glow with happiness, love, and kindness.

Dear God, thank you for Jesus who makes us glow with happiness, love, and kindness. Amen.

32

Making It Shine

> **Text:** "For once you were darkness, but now
> you are light in the Lord; walk as children
> of light" (Eph. 5:8).
>
> **Object:** Light bulb, battery, water, and salt
>
> **Theme:** Christians add love to our world to
> make it shine for God.

We are going to do an experiment. How many of
you enjoy experiments? [*An enthusiastic response
should be in order. Children seem to love a good experiment.*] As you can see, I have a light bulb [*A small
bulb in a socket with wires attached such as the kind
used for model trains or dollhouses works best.*], a battery [*A six-volt battery with wire fasteners will serve the
purpose.*], a glass of water, and some salt.

If I take the wires attached to this battery and the
wires attached to this light and put them in the
water, do you think the light bulb will shine?
[*Responses should be mixed.*] Some of you are saying
yes and some of you are saying *no*. Let's do the experiment and see who is right. [*Put both sets of wires into
the glass.*] Does the light bulb shine? [*Allow the children to respond.*] No, the light bulb is not shining.
Suppose I put salt in this water. Do you believe *that*
would make our light bulb shine? [*Again, responses*

should be mixed.] Let's try it. [*Add a good amount of salt to the water.*] Is our light bulb shining? [*Allow the children to respond.*] Yes, the light bulb is shining. We have learned in our experiment that adding salt to water causes the light bulb to shine. Isn't that exciting?

Let me share something with you that is even more exciting! Jesus once said that we are the salt of the world. What he meant is that when we add our love to the world, like adding salt to this water makes our light shine, we can make our world shine. Nothing could be more exciting than making our world shine for God.

Let's ask God to help us add love to our world so we can make it shine for him.

Dear God, help us to add love to our world to make it shine for you. Amen.

33

Recipes for Living

Text: "All scripture is inspired by God and profitable for teaching, for reproof, for correction, and for training in righteousness" (2 Tim. 3:16).

Object: Cookbook

Theme: The Bible contains recipes for living.

How many of you have ever helped your mom or dad cook? [*Allow the children to respond.*] Tell me, what have you helped to cook? [*Allow the children to share. Reinforce by repeating the names of the dishes they have helped to prepare.*] My goodness, you have been a great help in the kitchen, making cakes, brownies, popcorn, pancakes, and cookies.

If you were to make a cake, how would you know what ingredients to use, and how would you know how to put the ingredients together? [*At least one child should mention using a cookbook.*] Right. A cookbook would be very useful because it would give you the recipe you need for making your cake. [*Open the cookbook to a cake recipe.*] This recipe shows us how many eggs to use, how much sugar is needed, and how long to bake the cake. If we follow the directions of this recipe, we will have a wonderful cake for dessert.

Just as cookbooks give recipes for cooking, the Bible provides recipes for our lives. There are many wonderful recipes that give us the right ingredients for living. [*Open your Bible. Marking the following verses beforehand will help.*] For example, the Bible tells us to "love one another" (John 13:34); "Be kind to one another" (Eph. 4:32a); and "Pray for one another" (James 5:16b). If you follow the directions of these recipes, you can be sure to have a wonderful life.

Dear God, thank you so much for giving us recipes for living. Amen.

34

Worthy of Study

Text: "But his delight is in the law of the Lord, and on his law he meditates day and night" (Ps. 1:2).

Object: Test

Theme: Spending time studying your Bible is very wise.

Those of you who are a little older will know right away what I am holding in my hand. [*Show the children a test. I recommend using a third-grade math test with the word* test *clearly written at the top of the sheet to make this object easily identifiable.*] Yes, this is a test—a math test. Some of you are already looking a little concerned, but don't worry; I am not going to give you this test today.

Suppose you were going to have a math test; how would you prepare for it? [*Allow the children to respond.*] Of course, you would be very wise to study. To prepare for this test you would need to study adding your numbers. The more time you spent practicing adding your numbers the better you would do on this test.

In Sunday school, we do not give tests like this one, but we do spend a lot of time studying the Bible. Can you tell me some of the things we study in the Bible? [*Allow the children to share. Reinforce their answers.*] Yes (Name), we study stories in the Bible. Yes (Name), we study famous people in the Bible like Jesus, Moses, and Noah. Yes (Name), we study the many ways God has shown his love for each of us.

Spending time studying your Bible is very wise. The more time you spend studying your Bible, the better you will understand what it has to say. That's important because the real test of how well you understand your Bible is how well you live every day of your life.

Dear God, may we have the wisdom to study the Bible. Amen.

35

Our Special Family

Text: "For whoever does the will of my
Father in heaven is my brother, and sister,
and mother" (Matt. 12:50).

Object: Mirror

Theme: We can love, support, play, and share
with one another as a family.

Boys and girls, please look into my mirror and tell
me what you see. [*Use a mirror large enough for all the
children to see themselves. The children will respond
quickly to this question.*] Of course, you see yourselves.
I can see that you like what you see! No wonder.
Looking into this mirror we see (Name) with his
beautiful brown curls, (Name) with her lovely smile,
(Name) with her pretty blue eyes, and (Name) with
his handsome red sweater.

Most importantly, what I see when I look into this
mirror is my church family. Did you know that you
are my church family? [*This thought will probably sur-
prise the children.*] You are. The Bible tells us that as
Christians we are like brother and sister and mother
and father to one another. That makes sense to me
because like a family, we love to play with each
other, share with one another, learn together, and
care for one another.

Having such a wonderful family is a special privilege. Every day I thank God for each one of you. Today I want you to thank God for your church family. Let's thank God that we can love, support, play, and share with one another as a family.

Dear God, thank you that we can love, support, play, and share with one another as a family. Amen.

36

Rules, Rules, Rules

Text: "You shall walk after the LORD your God
and fear him, and keep his command-
ments and obey his voice, and you shall
serve him and cleave to him" (Deut. 13:4).

Object: Rules

Theme: Rules help us do what is best for us.

How many of you have rules in your home? [*A
quick response should be forthcoming.*] Goodness, it
looks like everybody has rules in their homes. Tell
me, what are some of the rules in your home? [*Using
a magic marker, write a few of the rules given by the children on a poster board.*] "Wash your hands before you
eat." "Don't hit your sister." "Don't play in the
street." "Do all your chores." "Do your homework
before playing."

Why do you suppose your mom and dad have
rules for you to follow? [*Children should point out that
rules help keep you safe and help you to do what is right.*]
I see; following rules helps keep you safe and helps
you to do what is right. Rules are an important way
for your parents to help you do what is best for you.

Did you know the Bible has rules? [*Some of the
children may be aware of the rules in the Bible.*] Can
you tell me any of the rules in the Bible? [*Using a*

magic marker, write a few of the rules given by the chil-
dren on a poster board underneath the home rules. If the
children cannot think of the Bible rules, suggest some
yourself.] "Do not kill." "Do not steal." "Do not lie."
"Honor your father and mother." Like following the
rules in your home, following the rules in the Bible
helps keep you safe and helps you to do what is
right. Bible rules are an important way for God to
help you do what is best for you.

Dear God, thank you for rules that help us do what is
best for us. Amen.

37

Bundle Up!

> **Text:** "The LORD will keep your going out and your coming in from this time forth and for evermore" (Ps. 121:8).
>
> **Object:** Warm coat
>
> **Theme:** God's love can make us feel warm all over.

When you go out to play these days, you probably hear your mom or dad reminding you to put on a warm coat. Why do you suppose wearing a coat is important? [*Allow the children to explain the importance of wearing a coat on a cold winter's day.*] Can you imagine what it would be like to go out today without a coat? [*Allow the children to describe how they would feel.*] Yes, within a few moments you would be freezing. Your teeth would be chattering and your body would be shaking all over. Without a coat, you would be miserable. However, if you are smart enough to wear a coat [*Put on the coat.*] you can keep warm no matter how cold it may be outside.

As miserable as it can be not wearing a coat on a cold winter's day, it can be even more miserable living our lives without God. Without God, we can feel very cold and lonely on the inside. But when we cover ourselves with God's love, it is like putting on a warm coat. No matter how cold, or lonely, or sad you may feel on the inside, God's love has a way of making you feel warm all over.

Dear God, thank you for your love that makes us feel warm all over. Amen.

38

Like the Wind

Text: "'But the Counselor, the Holy Spirit, whom the Father will send in my name, he will teach you all things, and bring to your remembrance all that I have said to you'" (John 14:26).

Object: Glider

Theme: We can know that God's unseen spirit is with us.

Probably every one of you, at one time or another, has played with a glider airplane. Can one of you tell me how this glider works? [*Allow a child to explain.*] Exactly. Working a glider is very simple. All you do is hold the glider like this and throw it into the wind. Then the plane glides. Can anyone tell me why the plane glides through the air? [*Allow a child to explain. If none of the children know why, continue with the explanation.*] I see; the glider is floating on the wind. How do you know that it is floating on the wind? Can you see the wind? [*A quick* no *should be forthcoming.*] If you cannot see the wind, how do you know it is there? [*Allow the children to explain.*] I see; you can feel the wind. And the wind that you feel is what the glider flies on.

Many times in church you may hear us talking about the Spirit of God. The Spirit of God is much like the wind that this glider flies on. No one has ever seen the Spirit of God, but many of us have felt God's Spirit. Like feeling the wind, we can know that God is with us, even though we cannot see him. As much as this glider can trust the wind to be there to glide on, we can trust God's Spirit to be with us.

Let's thank God for the presence of his Spirit.

Dear God, thank you for the presence of your Spirit. Amen.

39

Safe and Secure

Text: "Thy word is a lamp to my feet and a light to my path" (Ps. 119:105).

Object: Night-light

Theme: Jesus makes us feel safe and secure.

I have something with me that many of you use every night. Can anyone tell me what this is? [*Allow the children to respond.*] Right. This is a night-light. How many of you use a night-light when you go to bed? [*Allow the children to respond.*] Why do you use a night-light? [*Allow the children to share various reasons.*]

I can remember how important my night-light was to me when I was young. To tell you the truth I was a little afraid of the dark, just like some of you. Having the night-light on made me feel safe and secure because I could see everything in my room.

Now that I'm older, I don't use a night-light anymore. But I still need to feel safe and secure. Jesus is like a night-light; whenever I am afraid I can go to him. Jesus always makes me feel safe and secure because he is like a light that helps me see through the darkness,

I am so glad that we have night-lights to make us feel safe and secure. But, boys and girls, I am even happier that we have Jesus to make us feel safe and secure.

Dear God, thank you for Jesus who helps us feel safe and secure. Amen.

Someone to Listen

> **Text:** "A friend loves at all times" (Prov. 17:17a).
>
> **Object:** Teddy bear
>
> **Theme:** God will always listen to us and loves us no matter what we say or do.

What do I have with me? [*A quick response should be in order.*] Yes. That's exactly right. This is a teddy bear. How many of you have a teddy bear at home? [*Allow the children to respond.*] That's wonderful. Just about everybody has a teddy bear, and I bet those of you who don't have another special stuffed animal. Tell me, what do you like about your teddy bear? [*Children will provide a variety of answers. Allow them a few moments to share their thoughts and then continue.*] My teddy bear's name is Huggins. I love Huggins for many of the same reasons you said you love your teddy bears. I especially love Huggins because Huggins is my special friend who will always listen to me. Huggins loves me no matter what I say or do.

I know that God is my special friend who will always listen to me. And like a loving teddy bear, God loves me no matter what I say or do.

I'm happy we have teddy bears that will always listen to us whenever we need to talk and love us no matter what we do. But boys and girls, I'm even happier we have God who will always listen to us and loves us no matter what we do.

Dear God, thank you for always listening to us and loving us no matter what we say or do. Amen.

41

A Handful of Pennies

Text: "Finally, all of you, have unity of spirit, sympathy, love of the brethren, a tender heart and a humble mind" (1 Peter 3:8).

Object: Pennies

Theme: It is wonderful what happens when we all come together.

As you can see, I have a penny in my hand. What are some of the things I can buy with this penny? [*The children will have difficulty thinking of anything a single penny can buy.*] Unfortunately you are right. One penny will not buy much of anything. Do you think I should throw this penny away? [*Allow the children to respond.*] No? Why not? [*The children should point out that the penny can be used with other pennies to buy something of value.*] I see. I cannot use one penny to buy much of anything, but if I use this penny along with other pennies, [*Reach into your pocket and pull out a handful of pennies.*] I can buy a whole pack of gum, a candy bar, or even a toy. Isn't it wonderful what happens when you have a handful of pennies?

Like one penny needs other pennies, we need each other. For example, can one person play Duck, Duck, Goose? [*Allow the children to respond.*] Right.

We need each other to play Duck, Duck, Goose. Can one person be a whole family? [*Allow the children to respond.*] Of course not. We need each other to have our families. Can one person be our children's choir? [*Allow the children to respond.*] Absolutely not. We need each other to have our children's choir. Isn't it wonderful what happens when we all come together?

[*Give a penny to each child.*] Take your penny home and save it until you have collected enough pennies to buy something valuable. When you spend your handful of pennies, remember how wonderful it is when we all come together.

Dear God, help us to remember how wonderful it is when we all come together. Amen.

Making a Joyful Noise

> **Text:** "It was the duty of the trumpeters and singers to make themselves heard in unison in praise and thanksgiving to the LORD" (2 Chron. 5:13a).
>
> **Object:** Musical instruments
>
> **Theme:** There are many different ways to praise God.

As you can see, I have several different objects with me today. Can anyone tell me what this object is? [*Allow the children to respond.*] Right. This is a guitar. [*Strum the guitar.*] What is this? [*Allow the children to respond.*] This is a trumpet. [*Blow the trumpet.*] I'm sure you know this instrument, too. [*Allow the children to respond.*] Of course, this is a drum. [*Beat the drum.*] Can you name any other musical instruments? [*Allow the children to name a variety of musical instruments.*]

As we have heard today, different kinds of musical instruments sound different, but all musical instruments do the same thing. Can you tell me what they do? [*Allow the children to answer.*] Of course, all musical instruments play music.

Did you know that we are all here today for the same reason? We are here to praise God. Of course

94

there are many different ways to praise God. Can you tell some of the ways we praise God? [*Allow the children to respond, and summarize their answers.*] You are right. We can praise God by singing, by praying, by worshiping together, and by telling others about Jesus. When we praise God in many different ways, we become like different kinds of musical instruments that all join together to make music. In fact the sweetest music in the world comes when we all join together to praise God. Let's all join together right now and praise God through prayer.

Dear God, thank you for the many different ways to praise you. Amen.

43

Special Needs

Text: "He transplanted it to good soil by abundant waters, that it might bring forth branches, and bear fruit, and become a noble vine" (Ezek. 17:8).

Object: Seeds

Theme: If we are to grow and be healthy, we must have certain needs met.

Can anyone tell me what is inside this jar? [*Allow the children to respond.*] Right. These are seeds, but they are not of any use. You see, I put these seeds in my room for a whole month. Do you know what happened to my seeds? Nothing. They have done absolutely nothing. I was hoping they would grow into splendid plants with beautiful flowers. Unfortunately my seeds have not even begun to grow.

Maybe I am doing something wrong. Can you help me? [*The children should make several useful suggestions.*] I see. (Name) says I should plant my seeds in soil. What a great idea. Is there anything else I need? [*Allow the children to respond.*] Of course, (Name) is right. My seeds need water. And when my little plant begins to grow, it will need plenty of _____ (sunshine). What a smart group. You know exactly what my seeds need to be healthy and grow.

96

Seeds are not the only things that need care to grow. Like a seed, each of us starts life as a tiny baby. If we are to grow and be healthy, we must have certain needs met. Can you tell me what some of those special needs are? [*Allow the children to respond.*] You have given some wonderful answers. We need food, water, parents that love us, God's love, teachers, and kindness. Having these needs met will help us grow into beautiful persons, just like soil, water, and sunlight will help these seeds grow into beautiful flowers.

Dear God, thank you for meeting our needs so we can be healthy and grow. Amen.

How Big Is God's Love?

Text: "And to know the love of Christ which surpasses knowledge, that you may be filled with all the fullness of God" (Eph. 3:19).

Object: Numbers

Theme: God's love, like numbers, goes on and on, forever and ever.

How many of you can count to ten? Everybody. Good, let's count to ten together. [*Count to ten with the children.*] Does anyone know a number bigger than ten? [*Allow a child to respond and continue with the number given.*] Yes (Name), one hundred is much bigger than ten. How about a number bigger than one hundred? [*Allow a child to respond and continue with the number given.*] One thousand is much, much bigger. Can anyone think of a number bigger than one thousand? [*Allow a child to respond and continue with the number given.*] One million is a very, very big number. Maybe someone can tell me the biggest number in the whole, wide world. [*The children will venture answers to what they believe to be the largest number.*] You have given some great answers, but the truth is there really is no biggest number in the world. The reason there is no biggest number is because numbers go on and on and on, forever and ever. No matter what number you may think of, there is a number that is bigger because numbers never end.

The same is true when we think of how big God's love is for each of us. No matter how much we may believe God loves us, the truth is that he loves us even more. God's love, like numbers, goes on and on, forever and ever.

Let's thank God that his love for each of us never ends.

Dear God, thank you for your love that never ends. Amen.

45

Stuck Together

Text: "And lo, I am with you always, to the close of the age" (Matt. 28:20b).

Object: Glue

Theme: Jesus will stick with us all through our lives.

I'm thankful all of you are here this morning. I need some help. As you can see, I have several pictures that I have cut out of a magazine that I would like to keep on this sheet of poster board. But, every time I pick up the poster board, my pictures fall off. [*Demonstrate.*] What would be a good way to stick these pictures onto this poster board? [*Allow the children to respond.*] What a smart group! Of course, glue would do the job nicely. Thank goodness, I happen to have a jar of glue with me. [*Bring a jar of children's glue into view. Place a little glue on each picture. I recommend having about three pictures so that you do not use too much time gluing the pictures into place.*] This is great! Now my pictures are stuck onto the poster board. [*Demonstrate by picking up the poster.*] Wherever I take my poster board, I can be sure my pictures will be stuck to it.

Wouldn't it be wonderful if each of us was stuck to Jesus like these pictures are stuck to the poster board? That would mean that wherever we go, we could be sure that Jesus is with us. To tell you the truth, the good news is that that is possible. The Bible teaches us that Jesus will always be with us. We can be sure that wherever we go, Jesus will be stuck to us like a glue. That's wonderful, because with Jesus in our lives we truly can know real love and happiness. Let's thank God for Jesus who will stick with us all through our lives.

Dear God, thank you for Jesus who will stick with us all through our lives. Amen.

Special Days

Like a Rose

Valentine's Day

Text: "'As the Father has loved me, so have I loved you; abide in my love'" (John 15:9).

Object: Rose

Theme: We should love others not just for their good traits, but also with their bad.

If we were to take the time to ask everyone in our church what their favorite flower is, I am sure the rose would be one of the most loved flowers. Do you like roses? [*Allow the children to respond.*] What do you think is special about a rose? [*Allow the children to share the special qualities of a rose such as smell, color, texture, beauty, and so forth, and reinforce each comment. For example, "I love the smell of a rose too." (Smell the rose and allow the children to smell it) or "Roses are special because of their bright colors. What are some of the colors you have seen in roses that you like most?"*] There are so many good things about a rose. Can you think of bad things about a rose? [*Children will point out the thorns.*] Yes. You must be very careful when holding a rose because the thorns can hurt you.

Do you think I should not love this rose because it has thorns? [*Children will point out that the rose can still be loved, even with thorns.*] Right. I still can love this rose even though it has bad things, like the thorns, because it also has good things, like the color and smell.

Like roses, people are both good and bad. Our friends can be very nice to us and they can also hurt us. But we still love them, just like we love this rose, even though it has thorns.

This Valentine's Day, tell those you love that you love them not just for their good, but also with their bad. When you do that you will be loving them just like God loves you.

Dear God, help us to love others like you love us. Amen.

What Makes a Good Mother?

Mother's Day

Text: "Train up a child in the way he should go, and when he is old he will not depart from it" (Prov. 22:6).

Object: Infant

Theme: Mothers need God's help to be good mothers.

Why do you suppose we brought babies into church today? [*Allow the children to respond.*] Yes, today is Mother's Day. On Mother's Day we remember in our families and our church the importance of being a good mother.

As you can see, one of our mothers is letting me hold her baby for each of you to see. His name is (Name). Let me tell you a little secret. (Name) is the first baby in his family. That means his mom has never been a mother before (Name) arrived. Would you all like to help (Name's) mother? [*Children should respond with an enthusiastic* yes.] You can help her by telling her some of the things she can do for (Name) to be sure she will do a good job as a mother. What are some of the special things (Name's) mother should do? [*Allow the children to respond. If they hesitate, ask a few questions. For example,* "What if (Name)

106

is hungry?"; or "What if he falls down?"; or "What if (Name) is sick?" and so forth.]

There really are a lot of things that (Name's) mother needs to do to take care of (Name). Being a good mother for (Name) is an important and very, very big job. On this Mother's Day let's ask God to help (Name's) mother and all mothers to do their very best in being good mothers.

Dear God, help (Name's) *mother and all mothers to do their very best to be good mothers. Amen.*

More than a Kiss

Easter

> **Text:** "For God so loved the world that he gave his only Son, that whoever believes in him should not perish but have eternal life" (John 3:16).
>
> **Object:** Hershey's Kisses
>
> **Theme:** Jesus loves each of us more than all the Hershey's Kisses in the world could show.

Of all the candies in the world, I do not believe there is one that I like any better than Hershey's Kisses. The only problem I have with eating a Kiss is that I am never satisfied with just one. Sometimes I even tell myself that I think I'll have just one, but I always end up eating two or three or maybe ten.

Second-best to eating Kisses is giving them away. Do you all like Hershey's Kisses? [*An enthusiastic response should be forthcoming!*] Great. [*Hand out some Hershey's Kisses and continue.*] Knowing how much I love Hershey's Kisses and then seeing how much you love Hershey's Kisses, makes me feel like I am giving a little bit of love away every time I hand you a Kiss. That's why I love sharing them.

On Easter Sunday we think a whole lot about the love Jesus shares with us. When I think of Jesus' love I know that we could fill this entire sanctuary from top to bottom with Hershey's Kisses and all those Kisses would not come close to showing how much Jesus loves you.

Enjoy the Kisses I gave to you this morning. Remember they are my way of sharing love with you. God's way of sharing love with us was by giving us Jesus who loves each of us more than all the Hershey's Kisses in the world could show.

Dear God, thank you for sharing love with us by giving us Jesus, who loves each of us more than all the Hershey's Kisses in the world could show. Amen.

Go and Tell

Easter

> **Text:** "And he said to them, 'Go into all the world and preach the gospel to the whole creation'" (Mark 16:15).
>
> **Object:** Helium balloons with Scripture verses inside
>
> **Theme:** Telling others Jesus has risen.

I can already see many of your eyes popping out as you look at my beautiful bouquet of green, blue, red, orange, purple, and yellow balloons. Tell me, what would happen if I let go of all of my balloons? [*Allow the children to provide the answer.*] Of course, the balloons would rise to the ceiling. Why is that? [*Allow the children to explain.*] Right. The balloons have helium inside. Helium is a gas that is lighter than air. So the helium makes the balloons go upward.

If you look closely, you will see there is something else inside each balloon. What else do you see on the inside? [*Allow the children to respond.*] Right. There is a piece of paper inside every balloon. Each piece of paper has the words "Jesus has risen" and a Bible verse. The Bible verse is from the Gospel of Mark and shares the words of Jesus: "Go into all the world and preach the gospel to the whole creation."

Because today is the day we remember Jesus' rising from the dead, we will celebrate by allowing each of you to take a balloon outside where you can let it rise into the sky. [*The best time to do this is immediately following your worship service. At that time, the adults and children can gather to watch the balloons rise. Distribution of the balloons could occur at this point in the service or you may want to wait and distribute them following the worship service.*] Whoever finds your balloon will also find the Good News of Jesus written on the paper inside.

Let's thank God for this Easter Sunday when we celebrate Jesus' rising from the dead.

Dear God, thank you for Jesus' rising from the dead. Amen.

50

The Best Gift

Advent

> **Text:** "You shall love the Lord your God with all your heart, and with all your soul, and with all your mind, and with all your strength" (Mark 12:30).
>
> **Object:** Christmas and birthday cards
>
> **Theme:** The best gift you can give to Jesus is yourself.

[*Showing the birthday card, ask the following question.*] Can anyone tell me what kind of card this is? Of course, this is a birthday card. Tell me, what do you like most about celebrating a birthday? [*Allow the children to respond. You should receive a variety of answers including eating cake, playing games, and opening presents.*] I love going to birthday parties too. It's fun to play games, eat cake, and open presents.

Let me show you another kind of card. What kind of card is this? [*Allow the children to respond.*] Right. This is a Christmas card. Have you ever thought that Christmas cards are really birthday cards? Whose birthday are we celebrating? [*Allow the children to respond.*] Of course, we are celebrating Jesus' birthday. Celebrating Jesus' birthday can be as much fun as celebrating a friend's birthday. We can celebrate

Jesus' birthday by having parties, eating cake, playing games, and opening presents.

What do you suppose would be the best present you could give to Jesus? [*Allow the children to suggest some ideas. At least one child should mention that giving yourself (or your heart) is the best present to give Jesus.*] The best gift you can give to Jesus is you. When you give yourself to Jesus you will surely do all the things that will make him happy. Let's ask God to help us give the very best Christmas present of all—ourselves.

Dear God, help us to give you the best Christmas gift of all this year. Help us to give ourselves to you. Amen.